PIANO · VOCAL · GUITAR

RIHANNA · L

Due to licensing restrictions, "Fading" is not included in this folio.

ISBN 978-1-4584-0000-0

HAL·LEONARD®
CORPORATION
7777 W. BLUEMOUND RD. P.O. BOX 13819 MILWAUKEE, WI 53213

Visit Hal Leonard Online at
www.halleonard.com

S&M

Words and Music by MIKKEL ERIKSEN,
TOR ERIK HERMANSEN, SANDY WILHELM
and ESTHER DEAN

Recorded a half step lower.

WHAT'S MY NAME?

Words and Music by MIKKEL ERIKSEN,
TOR ERIK HERMANSEN, AUBREY GRAHAM,
ESTER DEAN and TRACY HALE

Additional Lyrics

Rap: Yeah, I heard you good wit' them soft lips. Yeah, you know word of mouth.
The square root of sixty nine is eight somethin', right? 'Cause I been try'n' a work it out, aaahh.
Good weed, white wine. Uh, I come alive in the nighttime. Yeah, okay, way to go.
Only thing we have on is the radio. Let it play. Say you gotta leave but I know you wanna stay.
You just waitin' on the traffic jam to finish, girl. The things that we could do with twenty minutes, girl.
Say my name. Say my name. Wear it out. It's gettin' hot, crack a window, air it out.
I could get you through a mighty long day. Soon as you go, the text that I write is gon' say...

CHEERS
(Drink to That)

Words and Music by ANDREW HARR,
JERMAINE JACKSON, STACY BARTHE,
AVRIL LAVIGNE, LAURA PERGOLIZZI,
ROBYN FENTY, SCOTT SPOCK,
LAUREN CHRISTY, GRAHAM EDWARDS
and COREY GIBSON

Moderate Hip-Hop groove

Yeah, yeah, yeah, yeah, yeah, yeah, yeah, yeah, yeah, yeah, yeah, yeah.

Cheers __ to the freak - in' week-end, I drink __ to that yeah, __ yeah. __

Oh, __ let the Jam-e-son sink in, I drink __ to that yeah, __ yeah. __

Ray - Bans on and I'm feel-in' hell - a cool to - night, ___ yeah. ___

Ev - 'ry - bod - y's vib - in' so don't no - bod - y start a fight, ___ yeah. ___

Cheers ___ to the freak - in' week - end, I drink ___ to that ___ yeah, ___ yeah. ___

Oh, ___ let the Jam - e - son sink in, I drink ___ to that ___ yeah, ___ yeah. ___

ONLY GIRL
(In the World)

Words and Music by MIKKEL ERIKSEN,
TOR ERIK HERMANSEN, CRYSTAL JOHNSON
and SANDY WILHELM

Dance Pop

CALIFORNIA KING BED

Words and Music by ANDREW HARR,
JERMAINE JACKSON and PRISCILLA RENEA

Moderate Power Ballad

Just when I felt like giv-in' up on us,

you turn a-round and give me one last touch.___ That made ev -'ry-thing feel bet - ter___

MAN DOWN

Words and Music by SHONTELLE LAYNE,
THERON THOMAS, TIMOTHY THOMAS,
SHAMA JOSEPH and ROBYN FENTY

Moderate Reggae feel

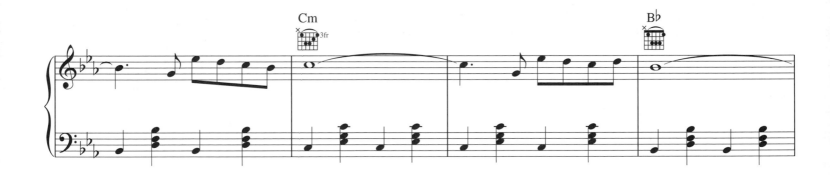

Ma-ma, I just shot a man down in Cen-tral Sta-tion.
(Sing 1st time only)

Repeat and Fade

Optional Ending

RAINING MEN

Words and Music by THERON THOMAS,
TIMOTHY THOMAS, ONIKA MARAJ,
MELVIN HOUGH II and RIVELINO WOUTER

Moderate Hip-Hop groove

Een-ie, meen-ie, min-ie, mo. Catch a play-a by the toe.

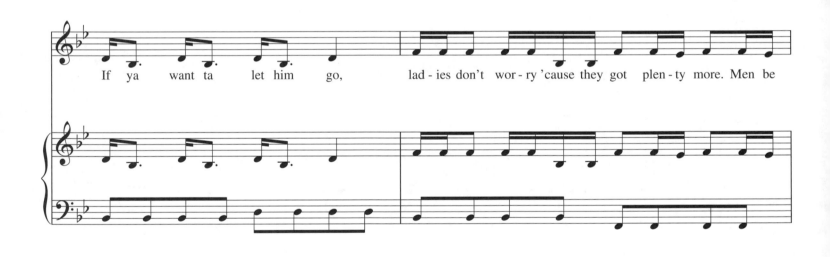

If ya want ta let him go, lad-ies don't wor-ry 'cause they got plen-ty more. Men be

fall-in' like the rain so we ain't run-nin' out. Fall-in' like the rain so we ain't run-nin' out.

D.S. al Coda

Men be

CODA

Fsus   Gb   N.C.

yeah, _ yeah, _ yeah, _ oh, _ oh, _ oh, _ oh. _   I said, "Hey, out-ta my way."   With my la-

Additional Lyrics

Excuse me but who are you fixin' to be.
Let them muthafuckas know it's plenty fish in the sea.
And he sweatin' me just 'cause I got the tightest hole.
But I couldn't find that th-thing wit a microscope.
Give me dome, dome, d-d-d-d-d dome, dome, dome.
I ain't trippin on yo honey, money long, long, long.
Want my own TV production company.
So tell Harpo to hit me Celie.
Anyway RiRi what rhymes wit yo name freely.
Money got you vacationing in Chile.
Do you want to sit on the bike while I wheelie, really, really?
Nah, for real, really?
Laid out on the beach they be feedin me my catfishes.
'Cause it's raining men fat bitches.

COMPLICATED

Words and Music by ESTHER DEAN
and CHRISTOPHER STEWART

Moderate Electro-Ballad

You're not ea-sy to love. _ You're not ea-sy to love, _ no. _

You're not ea-sy to love, _ you're not ea-sy to love, _ no. _ Why is

ev-'ry-thing ___ with you _ so com-pli-cat - ed? Why

Some-times I love you, _____ some-times it's you I can't stand. Some-times I want to hug you, some-times I want to push you a-way. _ Most times I want to kiss you, oth-er times put you in your place. _ 'Cause ev-'ry min-ute you _ start switch-ing up _ and you say things like _ you don't give a fuck. _ Then I

SKIN

Words and Music by KENNETH COBY,
ROBYN FENTY and URSULA YANCEY

Moderate groove

The mood is set, ha, ha, so you al-read-y
Al-most _ there, ha, ha, so ba-by don't

know what's next, uh, huh, uh.
stop what you're do-in', uh, huh, uh.

T-V on blast, turn it down, turn it down. Don't_
Soft-er than a moth-a boy, I know you wan-na touch. Breath-

_ want it to clash with my bod-y scream-in' out. Now,_ I know you hear-in' me.
-in' down my neck, I could tell you wan-na._ Now,_ and now you want it like.

Ha,_ you got me moan-in' now.
Ha,_ want you to feel it now.

I got a sec-ret that I wan-na show you, ooh.

LOVE THE WAY YOU LIE
(Part II)

Words and Music by ALEXANDER GRANT,
MARSHALL MATHERS III
and HOLLY HAFERMANN

Moderate Pop Ballad

On the first day of our sto- ry, the fu- ture seems so bright.

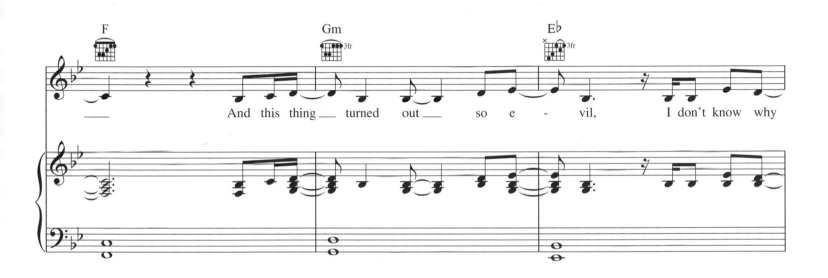

And this thing turned out so e- vil, I don't know why I'm still sur- prised.

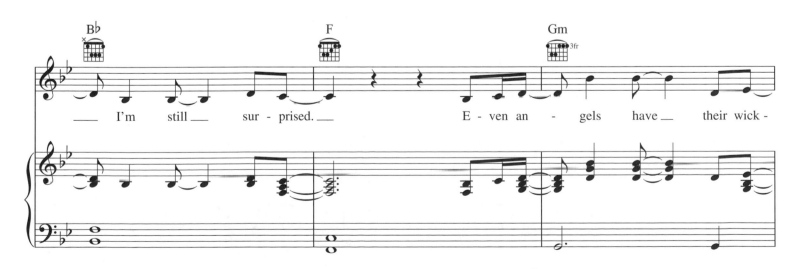

E- ven an- gels have their wick-

'til the walls ___ are go-ing up in smoke with all our ___ mem-o-ries. _____

___ Rap: *(See additional lyrics)*

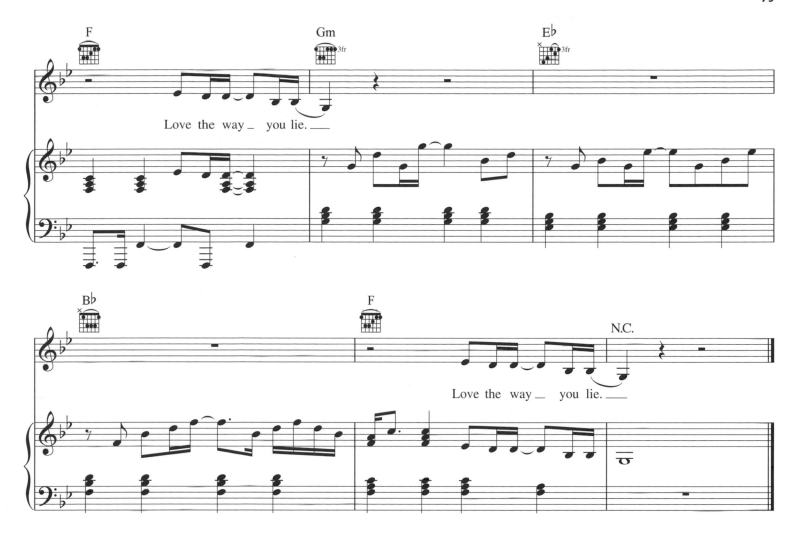

Love the way __ you lie. __

Love the way __ you lie. __

Additional Lyrics

Rap: This morning, you wake, a sun ray hits your face; smeared makeup
As we lay in the wake of destruction.
Hush, baby, speak softly, tell me you're awfully sorry that you pushed me
Into the coffee table last night so I can push you off me.
Try and touch me so I can scream at you not to touch me,
Run out the room and I'll follow you like a lost puppy.
Baby, without you I'm nothing, I'm so lost, hug me,
Then tell me how ugly I am, but that you'll always love me.
Then after that, shove me, in the aftermath of the destructive path we're on,
Two psychopaths, but we know that no matter how many knives we put
In each other's backs, that we'll have each other's backs 'cause we're that lucky.
Together, we move mountains, let's not make mountains out of molehills.
You hit me twice, yeah, but who's counting?
I may have hit you three times, I'm starting to lose count, but together,
We'll live forever, we found the youth fountain.
Our love is crazy, we're nuts, but I refused counseling.
This house is too huge, if you move out I'll burn all two thousand
Square feet of it to the ground, ain't shit you can do about it.
With you in my fucking mind, without you I'm out of it.